THE GUIDE TO SURVIVING NONSENSE: A SATIRICAL MANUAL FOR ADULTS TIRED OF B*LLSH*T

MILA ILKOVA

New York

All Books by the Author

Рассказать другу

Теория мудака

Пароль: Сарафан

New Yorkers Hate Food

Ой, всё!

Ten Myriad Moves

Rejection Letters of Book Agents

Mediamorons

They Said It's True

Rejection Letters of Future Employers

The Guide to Surviving Nonsense

MILAILKOVA.COM

Introduction

Congratulations on picking up this book. It's nice to know someone still reads in a world of seven-second attention spans. That is also how long it takes to check someone out and decide whether you'd fuck them. Well, at least we'll reproduce to survive. What comes after reproduction and how to survive all the nonsense — here's the satirical manual.

This book will embrace satire to tackle serious frustrations, mocking the absurdities of modern life while offering sarcastic, yet secretly profound, advice. Its goal is to inspire through humor, turning cynicism into a rebellious form of hope.

Hey, human! You good?

Humanity Factor

You thought it was just bad luck? Think again, Love. And recognize universal absurdities. Humanity thrives on chaos: reality TV shows, social media arguments, and small talk about the weather—the famous icebreakers meant to lead to long and meaningful relationships. They don't, obviously.

The majority of societal behaviors make people want to scream: endless meetings, unsolicited opinions, and pyramid schemes disguised as self-care. It's just who we are. Accept that.

Remember, everyone else is as confused by life as you are. Except they hide it way better, or have dream boards on Pinterest labeled "Adulting Goals," or pretend they know how to heal through herb picking and tea sipping.

Life would be a dream if it weren't for... other people. The absurdity is that without people, you wouldn't be able to hate people. And let's be completely honest: without people, you'd be bored.

If you've picked up this manual, chances are you're neck-deep in nonsense: contradictory emails at work, unreadable assembly instructions, "urgent" notifications from apps you don't remember installing, group texts that never end, unsolicited life advice from random acquaintances, and that neighbor who insists their parrot knows quantum physics. Take a deep breath—this book is here to guide you through all this. If you can laugh at the absurdity of the nonsensical behaviors of modern humanity, you've already won. And if not, well, there's wine for that.

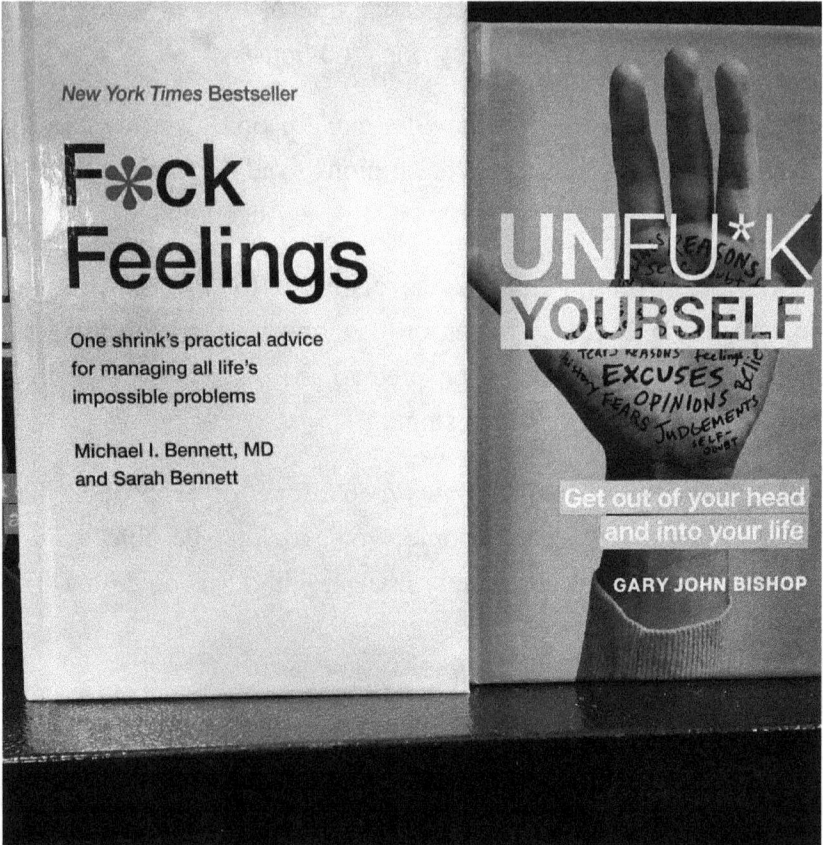

To f*ck or to unfu*k?
That is the question.

The Origins of Nonsense

You probably thought the nonsense in your life was just random chaos—an unfortunate byproduct of living among humans. Wrong. The truth is far more sinister. The nonsense in our lives is orchestrated by shadowy forces intent on making us lose our minds.

The world's nonsense isn't accidental. Neither is Karen's unsolicited opinion, nor a social media influencer holding a "Live, Laugh, Love" neon sign, nor a bureaucrat drowning in forms stamped "Rejected." It's all engineered. Every unnecessary meeting, every infuriating email, every conversation that starts with, "*I don't mean to be rude, but...*"—it's all part of a coordinated effort by a shadowy organization: the Bureau of Nonsense (BoN).

Yes, the BoN exists. And no, they don't wear cloaks or hold secret rituals (although they probably would if they could fit it into their busy schedule of making life harder for everyone). They're the invisible hand behind the world's most irritating events, ensuring that absurdity reigns supreme.

This book is your classified manual for uncovering, mocking, and defeating the Bureau of Nonsense—the secret organization behind all the absurdity in modern life. You need a survival dossier for navigating this lunacy with humor, defiance, and possibly tinfoil hats. Your mission? Survive their chaos, disrupt their plans, and laugh at their ridiculousness. Or else I have no other explanation for why nonsense exists and why we, as humans, complicate our own lives for the sake of nothing.

The Founding Fathers of Nonsense

Let's go back to the beginning. The Bureau of Nonsense was allegedly founded centuries ago during a dark, confusing time in history: the invention of bureaucracy. Somewhere between the creation of the first tax forms and the first committee meeting, a group of highly mischievous minds realized that they could weaponize inefficiency, confusion, and stupidity for their own amusement.

Ancient legends say the original BoN agents were responsible for the following:

Convincing the Romans that building aqueducts was more important than inventing indoor plumbing.

Adding silent letters to the English language (seriously, why is there a "k" in *knife*?).

Creating the first medieval town crier who shouted *"Hear ye, hear ye!"* — a phrase that meant absolutely nothing.

Convincing people to wear powdered wigs and waaaaay too much perfume instead of showering.

These pioneers of nonsense paved the way for the organization we know today.

Their motto? *If it doesn't make sense, make it louder!*

The Rise of Modern Nonsense

The BoN truly flourished in the 20th century, when nonsense became easier to distribute at scale. The invention of email, social media, and corporate buzzwords gave them the tools they needed to infiltrate every aspect of daily life.

Take, for example, corporate jargon. Did you think phrases like "Let's touch base," "Moving forward," and "Low-hanging fruit" happened organically? Absolutely not. These were painstakingly crafted in BoN laboratories by agents in business casual, all while sipping overpriced lattes and laughing maniacally.

A video blogger with a massive following frustratedly broadcasts a three-hour-long essay titled *"Why the Earth is Flat: A Defense."* Meanwhile, a BoN agent cackles in the background.

Unskippable YouTube ads and unsolicited pictures of people's babies are illustrations of a proud BoN agent wearing imaginary medieval knight armor, patting himself on the back for successfully executed madness. He was promoted to Head of the Foolery Department after this assignment. Fucker.

And don't even get me started on social media. The Bureau took one look at all of them and said, *"Yes. This will be our masterpiece."* Algorithms were designed to ensure that nonsense always rose to the top. Think of every viral trend that made you want to throw your phone out the window—planking, the Ice Bucket Challenge, blue dress/white dress madness. Classic BoN handiwork. Or that time everyone decided to buy Bitcoin, or sell Bitcoin, or brag about Bitcoin, or shut up about Bitcoin like it's an STI.

Why Nonsense Persists

You might think people surely see through this. But no. The BoN has mastered the art of making nonsense feel normal. Over time, humanity has simply accepted absurdity as a fact of life. We grumble about it, meme about it, but ultimately, we comply.

Why can you get a university degree online, but try renewing your driver's license without sacrificing a day and your soul?

Why do smartphones have more power than the computers that landed people on the moon, yet autocorrect still thinks you meant to say "ducking"?

Why are calories from a donut considered evil, but the same amount of sugar blended into a $9 smoothie with "antioxidants" considered health food?

Why do job listings require five years of experience for entry-level positions, but the people writing them seem to have zero experience using logic?

Why do airlines weigh your luggage down to the gram, but let people carry emotional support ponies on board?

Why do we buy expensive noise-canceling headphones to escape noise, but then blast music or podcasts so loud we basically recreate the noise inside our own heads? Silence is apparently the real luxury—and also the scariest thing to face.

These inconsistencies exist because someone, somewhere in the BoN decided it was funny to watch people argue. This is how the Bureau stays in power.

The Endgame of Nonsense

What does the Bureau of Nonsense ultimately want? It's simple: to keep us distracted, frustrated, and too busy dealing with everyday nonsense to ever stop, ask real questions, or challenge the status quo. Every time you spend an hour on hold with customer service or argue with a stranger online about pineapple on pizza, they win. But here's the twist: nonsense isn't just a tool for control. It's also their entertainment. Somewhere, in a secret underground bunker, BoN agents—the orchestrators of chaos—are watching your life unfold like their favorite sitcom. And they're not just analyzing your reaction to being charged $3.99 for an app you never downloaded—they're laughing at it. To them, your life is content. That meltdown over the broken coffee machine? Season 2, Episode 4. That long-winded email thread where nobody answers the actual question? Bonus material. That argument with a stranger about whether cereal is soup? Peak drama. The genius of the Bureau's strategy lies in its invisibility. Nonsense is so ingrained in daily life that we've stopped noticing it. We accept contradictory instructions, nonsensical policies, and logic-defying bureaucracy as normal. It's not. It's all by design.

The endgame isn't to break society—it's to stall it. To keep our cognitive bandwidth maxed out with trivia and frustration so we never quite get around to tackling the big stuff. Structural injustice. Environmental collapse. Systemic corruption. You know, the real plot lines. The good news: awareness is resistance. Every time you recognize nonsense for what it is, you disrupt the signal. Every time you choose clarity over chaos, you chip away at their foundation. Because the only thing the BoN fears more than order... is meaning.

What Can You Do?

The first step to fighting nonsense is recognizing it for what it is: deliberate, ridiculous, and utterly unnecessary. This chapter has equipped you with the truth. The question is, what will you do with it?

Spoiler alert: If your answer involves "submitting a formal complaint" or "starting a change.org petition" congratulations— you just got played by the BoN.

It is organized nonsense, after all, just like the mafia. And you have to know their tactics first.

Where nonsense spreads faster than wildfire.

What they do so you feel like trying to run fast in your nightmare.

The specific weapons of mass distraction, from corporate jargon to annoying TikTok trends.

Up next: Know your enemy. **Tactics of Organized Nonsense.**

Stay tuned. I'll be back after a quick commercial break.

Just kidding, there's no commercial break—it's a book.

Let's have a tea break.

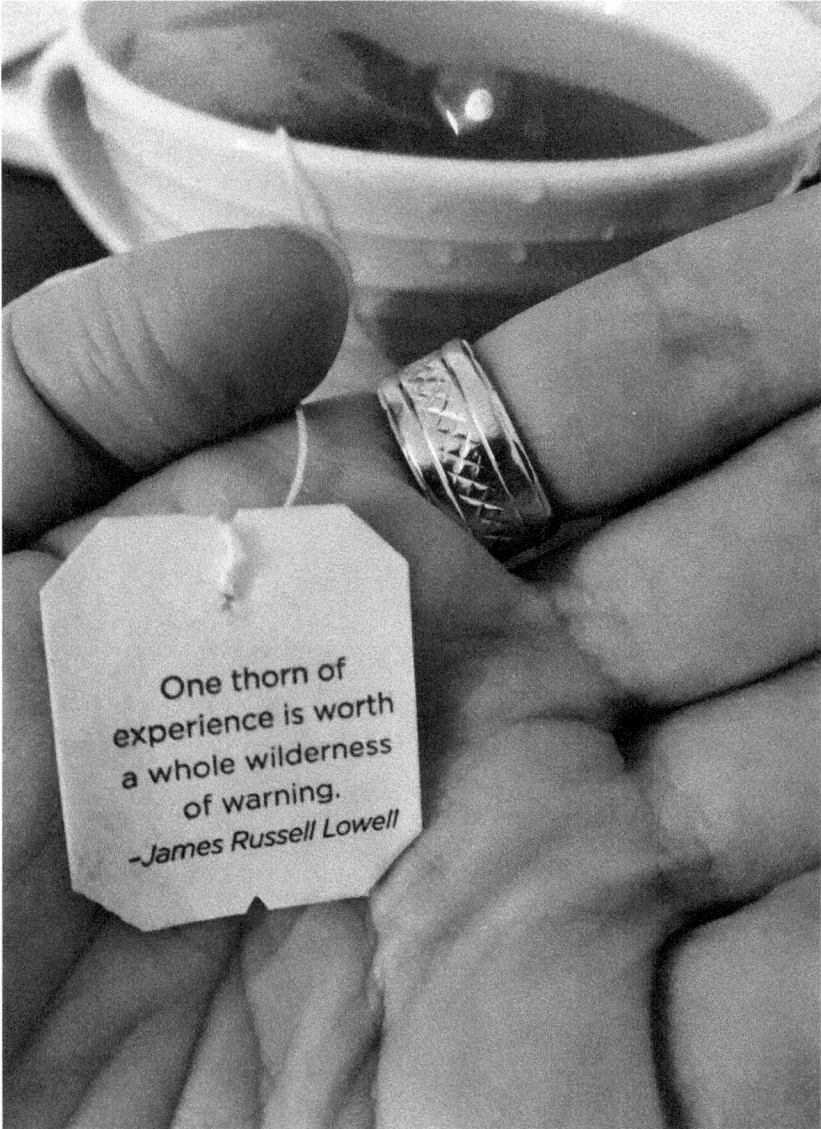

One thorn of experience is worth a whole wilderness of warning.
-James Russell Lowell

Love, have a cup of tea and think about what makes you smile.

*Tea, cup, water, electricity, golden ring, modeling palm and more inspirational quotes are all for sale.

15

Cookies or boobs? Boobs or cookies? Real cookies and fake boobs or real boobs and fake cookies?

The Art of Nonsense Detection

The first step to surviving nonsense is identifying it. Nonsense comes in many flavors, from mild confusion ("Do I really need a subscription for a toaster?") to full-blown absurdity ("Why does one take a thumbs up emoji as an insult?"). Equip yourself with the bullshit detector, applicable to all their tactics.

Smell Test: Does it stink of over-complication?

Logic Test: Could a six-year-old explain this better?

Gut Test: Does this make you question humanity's survival?

Tactics of Organized Nonsense

The Bureau of Nonsense (BoN) thrives on chaos and baffling the masses, ensuring you feel too overwhelmed to resist.

BoN operates with surgical precision, ensuring that nonsense becomes an unavoidable part of life. Their mission? Keep the world in a perpetual state of confusion and frustration.

These tactics are carefully engineered to exhaust your critical thinking skills, leaving you vulnerable to their nonsense. Below are the primary tools in their weapons of mass distraction arsenal.

Mass Confusion

Ever tried reading the terms and conditions for anything? Every pop-up that says, *"Cookies help us improve your experience,"* when you know darn well it's tracking your every move.

Or requiring you to share both your physical and mailing address.

Or telling you that they know your mother's maiden name better.

Or telling you that your password is not strong enough. So are my abs. Leave me alone; it is what it is.

Or by adding the word *experience* everywhere, especially where it's completely unnecessary.

"Subscribe to see my experience with Italian cuisine."

"This drug experience will change your life forever."

"Death experience is the only experience you won't remember."

Survival Tip: mess up with the messer!

"If I mention my full address, I'll expect holiday cards all year round. So I'm just avoiding frustration from unmet expectations. Here you go — City: New York, Street: New York, Apartment Number: New York, Zip Code: New York." There!

Weaponizing Small Talk

The BoN infiltrates conversations by training agents to say the most inane things possible.

"How about this weather, huh?"

"Yes, perfect for the uprising. They say revolutions love a good snow day."

"You wouldn't believe how long it took me to find parking!"

"My therapist thinks I should only leave my car in emotionally available spaces now."

"Have you heard about my keto journey?"

"No, but I hope it involved bacon."

"How was your weekend?"

"Productive. I reorganized my thoughts alphabetically."

"What do you do for fun?"

"Mostly I stare into the middle distance and narrate my life like it's a nature documentary."

<u>Survival Tip</u>: answer with honesty!

Mean it. Own it. Make the small talk big. If anyone asks how you're doing, actually answer how you're doing with full honesty — save on therapy.

Buzzword Bombs

Buzzwords are fluffy, vague terms dropped casually into conversations, meetings, and emails to sound important without saying anything meaningful. They are impossible to argue against without sounding like a caveman who doesn't "get it." Buzzwords succeed by making you feel inadequate. If you don't understand what they mean, you're conditioned to believe it's your fault—not that the person speaking is spouting nonsense. Once they drop the bomb, everyone in the room feels obligated to nod in agreement —the mass effect of organized nonsense.

"We're **disrupting** the industry!" Translation: "We're causing chaos, and we have no plan."

"Our teams need more **synergy**." Translation: "We're going to force people who hate each other to collaborate."

"He's a real **thought leader**." Translation: "He retweets articles without reading them."

"Let's be **agile**!" Translation: "Let's throw together random ideas and hope something sticks."

"Time to **pivot**!" Translation: "We have no idea what we're doing, so let's do something completely different!"

"We're **customer-obsessed**." Translation: "We ignore feedback but say 'thank you for your input' a lot."

"We're **scaling rapidly**." Translation: "Everyone's burned out and nobody knows who does what anymore."

"Let's **circle back** on that." Translation: "Let's pretend this never happened until someone forgets about it."

"We're **leveraging AI**." Translation: "We slapped 'AI' on it so investors would stop asking questions."

"We're creating a **disruptive ecosyste**m." Translation: "We built an app that breaks three things and solves one nobody asked for."

"We're **empowering** our employees." Translation: "We removed the coffee machine and added a Slack channel called #inspiration."

"It's part of our **innovation strategy**." Translation: "It was a wild guess, but we made a slide deck, so now it's official."

"I'm just really **focusing on myself** right now." Translation: "I don't want to commit to anything that requires pants or emotional effort."

"I'm **setting boundaries**." Translation: "I'm ghosting you with vocabulary I found on Instagram."

"I'm manifesting **success**." Translation: "I made a mood board and now I'm waiting for the universe to Venmo me rent."

"I'm on a **healing journey**." Translation: "I bought crystals and blocked three people. So far, so good."

"I'm **vibing** with the universe." Translation: "I quit my job, forgot to pay my bills, and now I'm blaming Mercury in Retrograde."

"I'm a highly sensitive **empath**." Translation: "I take everything personally and cry in Whole Foods over steak prices."

"I'm just being my **authentic** self." Translation: "Yes, I wore pleasers to brunch. No, I will not explain."

"I'm all about **balance**." Translation: "I spent three hours on a yoga mat and then ate an entire pizza. #FindYourZen."

"I'm just **going with the flow**." Translation: "I have no idea what's happening, but I've seen people on Instagram do it, so I'm pretending it's fine."

"I'm prioritizing my **mental health** and focusing on **positive energy**." Translation: "I'm blocking out negativity by ignoring my responsibilities and staying in bed to watch seven hours of Netflix."

"I'm **keeping my options open**." Translation: "I'm indecisive, but that sounds better than admitting I'm a commitment-phobe."

Survival Tip: reverse buzzwords!

"Let's amplify cross-functional growth by leveraging decentralized ecosystems!" This will either confuse the original buzzword dropper or lead to a chain reaction where everyone pretends to know what's happening.

Don't let them recover too quickly. Once you've dropped your buzzword bomb, pause, give them a confident look, and let the silence work its magic. Watch as they scramble to keep up, utterly confused by your audacity.

This technique works like a charm because it forces the nonsense-spewer into conceptual dissonance. Their mind can't process your counter-buzzwords because they're so far removed from their own jargon that it's like trying to solve a Rubik's Cube blindfolded.

When someone says, "We need to align," you hit back with a classic, "Let's quantum entangle instead. It's more efficient, and honestly, I think it's what the data is telling us."

Or when the dreaded phrase "synergy" emerges from someone's mouth like a dull, unwelcome fart in a meeting, shoot back with: "Synergy, huh? Let's just vibe and see if we can find some fractal resonance, too. I think that's the next level."

Love, have an extra cup of tea, because those buzzwords are so fucking annoying, I can't even...

The Creation of Pointless Conspiracy Theories

To create a pointless conspiracy theory, start with something random (like avocados) and make it sound overly complicated: "Avocados have bioelectric particles that track your movements when you eat guacamole." Add in some pseudo-science: "It's linked to quantum digestion and satellite signals." Spread it in forums and echo chambers with something like, "I heard it from an ex-CIA agent-turned-farmer." Layer on absurdity: "They're preparing us for the Great Avocado Reptilian War!" Then, make a wild prediction: "By 2045, the avocado conspiracy will be exposed." Millennials already eat avocados and ass, so who knows what the future holds for us.

<u>Survival Tip</u>: out-weird with your theory!

If yours sounds ridiculous enough, they'll lose track of their own nonsense.

"What about gluten-free bread? Are they in on it?"

Or simply admit you're an Earth-flatter and no one will ever tell you any conspiracy theory or even talk to you again.

Using Uneven Numbers in the Media in Listicles

Yes, it is also BoN's invention, as well as pretending a listicle is a legit article full of affiliate links and ridiculous writing.

"Breaking! You've Been Brushing Your Teeth Wrong Your Whole Life! HinT: It Should've Been Only 14 Times."

"6 Signs You're Not a Real Introvert And It's Your Fault!"

"Your Dog Is Probably Depressed Because You're Not Using This Special Water Bowl and Water for Dogs! 4 Bestsellers in May."

"9 Conspiracy Theories About Socks You Won't Believe, But the Truth Is Shocking."

"11 Things You Didn't Know About Your Refrigerator (But Should Have Known by Now)."

"How to Nap Like a Pro. 22 Techniques You've Been Doing Wrong. I'm a Sleep Expert and I've Only Been Using 16."

Survival Tip: approach with skepticism!

Before liking, sharing, or engaging, ask yourself, "Is this real or BoN-generated nonsense?" If in doubt, scroll past it — or better yet, close the app and go stretch.

The Social Media Swamp

The BoN found their most fertile breeding ground in social media, a digital cesspool where nonsense spreads faster than common sense. In this swamp, every trivial post, half-baked thought, and viral dance move becomes a weapon of mass distraction.

Outrage Algorithms. Social media platforms prioritize engagement through outrage. The more nonsensical or inflammatory a post, the more it gets shared. Rational debates get buried under an avalanche of hot takes and TikTok challenges.

Meme Wars. Memes, once innocent jokes, have evolved into weaponized nonsense. Entire discussions are reduced to a single image with text like "Can't adult today," effectively ending meaningful dialogue before it begins.

Influencer Absurdity. Influencers peddling nonsensical advice, from "manifesting success" by thinking positively to "cleansing your aura" with crystals, dominate the swamp. The BoN loves how this turns shallow trends into deep-seeming movements.

Survival Tip: log off and go for a walk!

Yeah, just that, Love. Enjoy nature.

Changing Words and Creating New Meanings

Words are no longer tools for communication, but emotionally reactive blobs that can be stretched, twisted, and redefined based solely on how someone feels that day. Reality is optional. Please adjust your speech accordingly, or be canceled with great emotional flair.

The Bureau of Nonsense thrives here.

Aggressive means *disagreed with me*.

Harmful means *slightly uncomfortable*.

And *literally* still means *figuratively*, but with more passion.

Survival Tip: buy a dictionary!

Carry it. Quote it. Slam it on the table. You can also (imaginarily) beat a meaning—fluid interpreter with the Merriam-Webster — a technique similar to imagining the crowd naked.

Pro level: imagine beating the entire naked crowd with the dictionary while they return to the only language reality for everyone.

Bureaucratic Quicksand

Bureaucracy is the BoN's most ancient and refined weapon. Over centuries, they've perfected a system where nothing is straightforward, and even the simplest task is a Herculean ordeal. Any institution with abbreviation letters in its title (DMV, HRA, USCIS, etc.) is the pinnacle of bureaucratic quicksand, where your soul dies a little with every wait in line. Their ultimate goal? Wear you down until you surrender. They know you'll lose the will to argue, because what other option do you have, really?

Every form, protocol, rule, and procedure is intentionally overcomplicated to the point of absurdity and contradiction.

Submit a form just to request permission to submit another form. One form requires your signature in blue ink, while another states that only black ink is acceptable. Or type only!

Need a refund? Fill out four different forms, scan your receipt, submit your request online, and wait eight to ten business weeks for someone to reject it due to a typo.

Would you like to unsubscribe from our service? No problem! Please submit your ID, SSN, DNA, and hair locks from your two most recent lovers by email to privacy@company.com. You will receive an email from noreply@company.com. Please don't reply. There is no one behind it. Not even a robot wants to talk to you. We will consider your request to unsubscribe within 90 days. Your data will surely be sold and shared everywhere.

Our corporate policy requires you to clock in digitally and on paper timesheets (for records), after you've already used your electronic entrance card with your name and photo ID on it.

Attend a meeting that could have been an email, only for the email to tell you there's another meeting.

Lost your ID? You'll need two forms of ID to replace your ID. And a birth certificate! Always have it ready just because even though it has no picture — a valid part of identification.

Need to open a bank account? We need your proof of address. Need to rent an apartment to have an address? You've got to have a bank account with the perfect credit score. Oh, but we won't open you a credit card to build your credit score. We will, though, open you a debit card and charge you monthly for not having enough money on it. You are very welcome.

Use our online form to schedule an appointment. This will prevent unnecessary lines. Our online appointment system's hours of operation are Monday through Friday from 9 a.m. to 12 p.m., excluding national holidays of all nations in the world. Oh, sorry, we have reached the maximum capacity for appointments for the next year. You need a paper form to submit it later to the infinite loop? Use our online form to schedule an appointment. This will prevent unnecessary lines.

Survival Tip: bring snacks and a podcast!

Perfect the art of persistence with sarcasm: "Oh sure, I'll resubmit the form. For the third time. No problem at all. Yes, I can spell my name again: M as in Mildly, I as in Irritated, L as in Losing, A as in Again."

Bureaucratic Infinite Loop

You're sent from one department to another in a never-ending cycle of referrals. If life feels like an endless loop of confusion and chaos, just remember: it's not you, it's the world. So grab this manual, a good laugh, and maybe some chocolate—because if nonsense is inevitable, you might as well thrive in it.

"We don't handle that here. You'll need to talk to Susan in Accounts."

To continue reading this paragraph, please go to **page 121** and follow instructions there. Go! Go!

You came back here from **page 79**. Repeat the process until you lose your mind. Congratulations, you've experienced a direct assault by the BoN.

<u>Survival Tip:</u> master the art of writing!

If you can't put it into words to send a message or email, there is no point in meeting! This tip will not solve the bureaucratic infinite loop, but it will save you a bunch of time on your commute, meeting with boring people who might have said their boring stuff via text message.

The Cult of Mandatory Positivity

Welcome to the happiest kind of hell, where the BoN forces everyone to smile like their lives depend on it—because in a way, they do. It's not about actually being happy; it's about pretending to be happy loudly, constantly, and with way too many exclamation points!!!!!!

You just got laid off? Wow, what a chance to reinvent yourself!
Your rent went up 40%? Time to manifest abundance!
Broke and anxious? Remember, the best things in life are free—like delusion and denial!

Toxic Affirmations. "Everything happens for a reason." Yes—sometimes the reason is someone in management made a spreadsheet mistake.

Sunset Quotes. If it's not on a pastel background with cursive font, is it even healing? "Gratitude is the new wealth!"—an Instagram influencer says while sipping green sludge with a link to $90 candles. #blessed #goodvibesonly

I am positive that things are awful. Positivity: ✅ Delivered.

Survival Tip: hit with radical authenticity!

You're not here to shine — you're here to survive with sarcasm. Bad day? Live through it, cry it out, reflect, and move on.

What Can You Do?

This is how the BoN keeps us all tangled in confusion and frustration—by overwhelming us with so many viral distractions, endless paperwork, and nonsense that we can't even begin to fight back. Their job isn't just to generate nonsense but to flood every corner of your life with it.

The BoN's tactics are relentless, but recognizing them is your first step to resistance. Once you see through the buzzword bombs, the social media swamp, and the bureaucratic quicksand, you'll start building the mental armor needed to survive this chaotic world.

Up next: How to **Recognize the Nonsense Agent** and protect yourself from their relentless attacks.

Stay tuned. I'll be back after a quick commercial break.

Just kidding, there's no commercial break—it's a book.

Let's have a tea break.

From a small seed
a mighty trunk
may grow.
-Aeschylus

Love, have a cup of tea and think about
what you would like to be known for.

*Tea, cup, water, gold ring and more inspirational
quotes are still for sale. Make an offer!

There's a fine line between real and fake, even though both might be the same. Learn the difference.

Recognize the Nonsense Agent

There are three types of Nonsense agents infiltrated into our everyday life. Their goal is to create chaos, forcing you to question reality.

All three agents interchange the departments to create even more chaos in our lives, so don't think that Karens are only found on Facebook or at stand-up clubs as hecklers and The Nonsense Machines are only deployed to annoy us at airports and offices.

Type 1. The Karen

Ignorant yet persuaded her opinion is the only correct opinion. Atrocious when involved in any human interaction, be it online, in real life, or in the wild. Typically recognized by bad haircuts and introduction phrases like "I don't mean to offend you but..."

Survival Tip: activate your CSV!

Customer Service Voice™ — calm, empty, and completely unbothered by logic: "Thank you for your very important feedback. I'll absolutely escalate this to the Department of Consequences." Bonus points if you call her Ma'am in a way that clearly means "Please evaporate."

Type 2. The Mediamoron

Specializes in mass media and social media nonsense. Often mimics fake for truth, truth for fake, and not important at all for very important, where it becomes almost impossible to differentiate one from another.

Typically just wants to "explore both sides," which always seems to mean defending the indefensible.

Calls anybody he/she doesn't like passive-aggressive, rude, offensive. Has the capability and resources to cancel anybody for anything or nothing at all—just for the hell of it.

Thinks he/she knows everything but, at best, can argue the moral upside of cargo shorts.

Survival Tip: fight fire with fire!

Use their own game against them — overwhelm with facts, satire, and irony. Ask endless clarifying questions until their contradictions tie themselves in knots. When cornered, they often retreat into vagueness or memes, so be ready to match absurdity with calm logic and intelligence.

Type 3. The Machine

The universal agent that is trained and equipped to complicate everything. Can mimic any type of agent. Extremely dangerous.

Master of ghosting and flaking. Always has big plans and promises, always super excited to hang out, but mysteriously disappears when it's time to follow through.

Adept at sending just "Hi" in a text message — and that's it.

Guru of wasting your time fueling fake overcommitment. Will keep telling you "yes" while the truth is "no," coming up with excuses why "no" can't become "yes," and making you wait a bit longer until you give up.

Pro of bragging. Favorite hobby is fishing — for compliments. No matter what you've done, they've done it better. Climbed a hill? They scaled Everest. Got a cold? They once had pneumonia *twice*. Their life is a competition, and they are winning. Except no one's playing.

Maestro of fake listening. Nods, smiles, says "Totally!" — but clearly didn't hear a single word and their eyes say "I'm thinking about bagels."

Chief of interruption. Listens only long enough to decide what *they* want to say next. Never heard a sentence they didn't want to hijack halfway through. Usually cuts you off before you finish a sentence. Talking to them is like trying to send a fax over a dial-up connection.

Warrior behind the keyboard. Online, they're a fearless debater. In person, they whisper their Starbucks order and apologize for existing. Big "I'll destroy you in the comments" energy.

Legend of being late. Time is a concept—an optional one. They will be late to their own funeral, and you'll still feel bad for mentioning it.

Ninja of complaining. Life is a never-ending series of personal tragedies, and you're the lucky soul they share all of them with. Everything is terrible and someone should do something. But not them. Never them. Got a paper cut? They'll tell you about the time they almost died from one. Emotionally. God forbid you offer a reasonable solution to any of the problems they complain about—they'll destroy you with a grimace of a victim.

Shaman of the close talk. No concept of personal space. Can and will breathe directly into your face. If you've ever tasted someone's breath without kissing them, blame this person. They're one "how's it going?" away from a restraining order. Worse than that is a stranger in line who is standing way too close, and you can feel the warmth of their breath at the back of your neck. Worse than that is when the stranger starts giving you advice.

Survival Tip: disengage immediately!

The one and only key to dealing with the Nonsense Machine Agent is to smile, nod, and say, "You're so right!" before promptly leaving.

Agents of Agents Who Thrive on Nonsense

The Bureau of Nonsense (BoN) is not some distant, shadowy cabal hiding in an underground lair. No, their genius lies in their stealth tactics—operating right in front of us, using ordinary people as unwitting agents of chaos. From the neighbors you see every day to the colleagues who fill your calendar with pointless meetings, these individuals are conduits of nonsense, infecting your life with irritation and confusion. Once you recognize them, you'll see them everywhere.

For some, nonsense isn't just a challenge; it's a way of life.

You know the devil's advocate type: the friend who texts you at 2 a.m. to debate the existence of aliens, or the colleague who starts every sentence with "Actually."

How do you recognize them? If you want to put somebody on an imaginary giant cactus—it's them.

The BoN hides in plain sight, using ordinary people as their agents.

If you can't spot one, congratulations... you might be one.

The Meeting Addict

The Meeting Addict thrives in offices, where they operate as one of the BoN's most effective agents. Their mission? Ensure no task can be completed without endless rounds of pointless discussions. They believe every minor issue requires a formal brainstorming session, complete with agendas, action items, a 90-minute Zoom call, and follow-up emails. They have never sent a single email in their lives that didn't need a follow-up meeting. These meetings suck time and energy from everyone involved, replacing productivity with mindless chatter. Their true purpose? To create an illusion of progress while ensuring nothing gets done. Typical behaviors include:

Stapler Summits. "Let's have a meeting to discuss the optimal stapler placement."

Endless Brainstorms. "I think we need another session to really 'unpack' this." Unpack what? No one knows.

Overzealous Scheduling. "Can everyone meet at 7 a.m. tomorrow? I feel we need to touch base ASAP."

Survival Tip: combat with absurdity!

Propose absurd meeting topics to highlight their ridiculousness: "Before we move forward, should we convene a quick subcommittee to discuss which font to use in our next email?"

The Pretend Philosopher

This agent believes they possess profound wisdom, but their actual insights come from random podcasts, social media influencers, or self-help gurus. Always ready to argue the worst possible perspective under the guise of "intellectual debate." Their mission? Spread pseudo-intellectual nonsense while making everyone around them question their sanity.

Quoting Joe Rogan or TikTok Influencers. They disguise these quotes as ancient wisdom. "You know, like Joe Rogan says, 'Life is just one big podcast episode.'"

Misusing Philosophy. "I think Kafka would agree that we should all manifest positive vibes in the workplace."

Signature move: "Well, actually"—readiness to correct you on anything, especially things that don't need correcting. They live to correct and thrive on technicalities. Will explain the origin of the word "literally." Well, *actually*, nobody asked.

Survival Tip: challenge with fascinating nonsense of your own!

"Did you know Aristotle also believed the moon was made of fermented cheese? Let's discuss that next." They'll either back down or engage until everyone walks away.

41

The Annoying Neighbor

Every building or block has one—the self-appointed deputy of decency, fluent in passive aggression and always ready to uphold rules no one agreed on. The BoN loves this type because they can turn minor inconveniences into moral crises faster than you can say "HOA violation." Their mission? Make you comply.

The Joy Dictator. They just can't stand when someone's having a good time. You watch TV—they hear the bass noise. You put decorations—they judge you for using too much electricity (that you pay for anyway). Your joy is unlicensed and must be removed.

The Surveillance Expert. They know who parks in your driveway, who visits you and what time, how many grocery bags you carried in, what packages you got delivered, and whether that was a DoorDash or a "suspicious visitor". They monitor all comings and goings—that's their investment in the community. And by "community," they mean your private life without your consent.

The Tap-Dancing-in-Heels Furniture Mover. Known for their 6 a.m. and 10 p.m. tap-dancing session in heels while dragging what can only be described as an iron cabinet across the floor for reasons unknown, while vacuum cleaning and drilling.

Survival Tip: agree with everything!

And do it your way. Nonsense is a game.

The Stranger With Advice

This is the person who appears out of nowhere—like a judgmental fairy godparent—armed with unsolicited life hacks, parenting tips, dating advices, career strategies, and strong opinions about your grocery choices.

Whether you're online or offline, a stranger with advice will find you anywhere. Whether you're too tall or too short, too fat or too skinny, too dumb or too dorky, married or single, with or without kids, walking, sitting, drinking, training, or keeping silent— there's always an advice for you.

They mean well. Probably. But their delivery system is part therapy session, part TED Talk, and part aggressive Yelp review of your life. "You didn't ask, but I delivered anyway."

Most strangers with advice don't stick around if they suspect *you* might start giving them advice. Eventually, they'll back away.

Survival Tip: throw them off balance!

The key isn't to fight them—it's to confuse them. Start giving them advice. Make it all about them. Mention your auntie who looked just like them and throw your arms ready for a hug and a kiss on the mouth. Give more advice in the meantime.

The Oversharer

Tells you about their DNA, emotional trauma, and toe fungus… in the first five minutes.

Way too much information, way too soon. You did not need to hear about their rash and a drama with their ex during your lunch.

Small talk? Never heard of it.

Survival Tip: share the unnecessary!

Make them feel the pain of your problems. And if they ask you how you're doing, answer in full with colorful details. Make them the godparent of your problems and never finish the conversation first. The ultimate goal is to outbid their oversharing, gaining the trophy of the oversharer yourself.

Where To Find Hidden Agents

While you can spot obvious agents, the BoN has infiltrated every corner of your daily life. They're everywhere, hiding in plain sight, working tirelessly to drain your patience. Knowing where to find them is the first step toward taking back control. They might be lurking in traffic, in stores, on Instagram, in parks, at concerts, in elevators, or just anywhere. Stay alert.

The Road. Lane weavers change lanes every five seconds, convinced their erratic behavior will magically clear congestion. BoN agents in disguise, their mission is to disrupt the flow and ensure everyone's commute feels like a nightmare.

The Street. People who stop in the middle of parking lot aisles to contemplate existence—or just to text—blocking everyone else from moving forward. Or in the middle of the street with rush hour pedestrian traffic to take a picture of the sky.

The Grocery Store. Confused line-cutter: *"Oh, I didn't realize this was the line!"* Some just stand there too close to you and you can feel their breathing onto your neck. So close! They also insist on interviewing the cashier as if it's *The Tonight Show* and argue every expired discount, making your quick errand an endless ordeal.

The Social Media. Armed with half-truths and conspiracy theories, these agents flood comment sections with nonsense, turning friendly conversations into battlegrounds or do it the Cold War style with endless inspirational quotes like, *"Live, laugh, love your best life today!"* Sounds innocent until your entire feed is flooded with BoN-approved clichés.

What Can You Do?

The BoN's greatest strength lies in its invisibility through normalcy. By embedding their agents into everyday roles and situations, they create a world where nonsense is normalized as part of life. But once you recognize their patterns, you can laugh in their faces and take your first steps toward nonsense liberation.

Up next: Learn how to deflect nonsense like a pro with survival strategies. Prepare your **Bullshit Shield**.

Stay tuned. I'll be back after a quick commercial break.

Just kidding, there's no commercial break—it's a book.

Let's have a tea break.

There is pleasure
in the
pathless woods.
-Lord Byron

Love, take a nap because you've
already had four cups of chamomile tea.

*The sale of tea, cup, water, electricity, modeling
fingers and more inspirational quotes can wait.

CATMAN
THE SUPERPOWER OF RRRMEOW

Love, like a real superhero, you can start your mission with coloring your superpower. It's like Scatman but cooler. Ski Ba Bop Ba Dop Bop.

*If you don't know who Scatman is, you're not tired enough to read this book, goodbye! Pass it to your mother.

Building Your Bullshit Shield

In the grand theater of life filled with an overwhelming amount of mind-numbing jargon, pointless meetings, useless tasks, passive-aggressive comments, and unsolicited opinions, your first line of defense is building a b*llsh*t shield. This isn't about being passive; it's about becoming a master of **deflection, distraction, and redirection**.

Chaos is often your greatest adversary, but it's also the perfect opportunity to fight fire with absurdity. There's only one thing to do: redirect that chaos back at them with the precision and elegance of a chaos maestro.

You see, there's power in making nonsense implode on itself. By turning the tables on the person throwing meaningless buzzwords or bad vibes your way, you not only gain the upper hand but you also send a clear message: this game is rigged, and you're not playing by their rules.

Confuse the BoN agents, make them scratch their heads in disbelief, become the hero who unleashes their next weaponized move.

With these techniques, you'll be able to navigate any conversation without losing your mind—or dignity.

Strategic Zoning Out

You know that moment when someone drops a buzzword salad on you and your brain just checks out? That's when you activate your strategic zoning out. Perfect the art of the blank stare, where you nod occasionally to give the illusion of engagement, but deep down, you've mentally wandered off to a better place. Maybe you're on a beach, or you're pretending to be in the middle of a secret spy mission, whatever it takes to survive the meeting.

Survival Tip: practice in front of the mirror!

You want the stare to be vacant enough to avoid any questions but not so blank that you look like you've just been lobotomized. It's a fine line between "I'm taking this seriously" and "I'm mentally on vacation."

Automated Replies

Ah yes, the beauty of automated replies is that you can still respond to all the nonsense without actually responding at all.

When someone sends you an email about some nonsense, hit them with the classic: "Thanks for your email. I'll get back to you never." It's concise, clear, and leaves no room for confusion.

You can always make it more elaborate: "Thanks for your email. Unfortunately, my schedule is currently booked with more important matters, like watching paint dry. I'll get back to you when Mars is in Venus making babies."

And more elaborate: "Thanks for your email. At the moment, my schedule is quite full with other pressing commitments and I'm currently navigating a rather full calendar of prior engagements. I'll be in touch as soon as the timing is a bit more favorable."

Survival Tip: ignore with art and flair!

I have received it with the enthusiasm of a cat at bath time. I am currently away from my desk, spiritually and emotionally. If your request is urgent, I suggest sitting quietly and reflecting on your life choices. Otherwise, I'll respond when I return and if I still remember who you are.

The Polite Pivot

Not everyone gets the memo about how ridiculous their conversation is. Enter the polite pivot, a smooth maneuver where you steer the conversation to safety by completely ignoring the absurdity and shifting focus to something more productive—or at least less soul-sucking.

When someone says something like, "We need to align our vision and touch base on the KPI deliverables for optimal traction," hit them with the ultimate polite pivot:

"Interesting thought! Totally aligned. Just need to recalibrate my third eye with a KPI spreadsheet made of donuts and whispered intentions."

It's the conversational equivalent of throwing a smoke bomb and disappearing into the fog. The goal is to keep things moving, even if it's away from a topic that makes your soul want to leave your body.

Survival Tip: practice the right timing!

The success of the polite pivot relies heavily on your delivery. If you do it too early, it can seem like you're avoiding the subject. If you do it too late, you'll come across as completely uninterested.

The Absurd Question

When confronted with utter nonsense, sometimes the best weapon is the absurd question. It's the perfect way to derail a conversation, turning the tables on the person bombarding you with nonsense.

"So, we're building this AI-powered, cloud-based solution for dynamic workflow optimization that also gamifies wellness by tracking your breathing in real time."

"Wow, that's amazing. Will it also scream at me if I exhale wrong? Or maybe unlock a bonus level if I manage not to bring up politics at the table?"

If someone decides to "care" and suggests you stop being single, lower your standards, or that the clock is ticking, ask them this: "Do you swallow or spit it out?"

Survival Tip: confuse and bewilder!

These questions are designed to force the nonsense-spouter to question their own absurdity. After all, they did bring it up in the first place. Repeat the line until they get the hint. Bonus points if you can do it in a tone that suggests they've just said the dumbest thing ever.

The Tactical Retreat

Sometimes, the best defense is a good offense. And by that, I mean exiting the conversation entirely without even trying to explain why. It's not always about winning the battle in the moment, but about saving yourself from an eternity of tedious nonsense.

The Tactical Retreat is a strategic move where you simply leave the room, the Zoom call, or the social gathering with no warning. This might involve slipping out the back door during a meeting, disconnecting from a video call mid-lecture, or—if you're feeling particularly bold—pretending to be urgently needed elsewhere.

"Oh, look at the time, I have to go cure world hunger—catch you later!"

"Gotta go. My phone is at 2%, and so is my will to engage."

Survival Tip: exit very dramatically!

This isn't about slipping away quietly, this is about making a statement. If you don't leave with at least three people wondering what just happened and a small group of onlookers staring in awe, you're not doing it right.

Confuse the Confuser

When confronted with passive-aggressive comments, your best defense is to go full throttle with a response that's so positive, cheery and supportive, it leaves the passive-aggressor perplexed and helpless. Enter the Confuse the Confuser technique.

"Oh, I love that journey for you! Your attention to detail is so inspiring. Seriously, it's like you're a productivity guru; it's an art form worthy of a masterclass."

"Ah yes, the delicate dance of intrusion and concern. You have such a unique way of saying nothing and everything all at once. I can feel the positive vibes radiating from your critique."

"Wow, your insight is truly groundbreaking. I'm amazed how you manage to be so engaged. Your comment really adds that special touch of sunshine to my day. I'll treasure it like a parking ticket."

Confused yet? You should be. By out-loving them with an overly supportive response, you rob them of their power to unsettle you. They expect you to react with defensiveness, anger, or guilt. Instead, you flip the script and show them that their attempt at aggression only fuels your unwavering optimism.

Survival Tip: sound sincerely positive!

The key here is sincerity. It will rattle them. After all, passive-aggressors thrive on negativity — they're allergic to cheerfulness.

Weaponized Humor

When all else fails, it's time to unleash the weaponized humor strategy. There's nothing more powerful than turning a frustrating situation into an absurd comedy show. If someone hits you with nonsense that's simply too dumb to take seriously, your best option is to laugh—but not just any laugh. You need a maniacal laugh that lets everyone know you're in control.

Your laughter is not just a reaction; it's a weapon. It's like pulling the pin from a grenade and watching the explosion of awkwardness that follows. This kind of humor is so disarming that most people will quickly realize they've walked straight into absurdity territory. At that point, your laughter has bested them, and they have no choice but to either back down or be laughed out of the room.

Timing is critical when deploying weaponized humor. Make sure the moment is as absurd as possible, and your laugh should come suddenly and loudly enough to catch them off-guard. The sheer audacity of your response will leave them speechless.

If the nonsense of life is a storm, humor is your umbrella—and maybe a cocktail in a travel mug. A good laugh is like a workout for your soul. Except no one's judging your form, and you won't pull a hamstring.

Survival Tip: celebrate humor as the ultimate survival tool!

Sunshine energy.

Spread the light or burn to death.

Use this tool wisely.

What Can You Do?

Building a bullshit shield isn't about shutting people down—it's about creating space for your sanity to survive.

Stand tall with a sword labeled "Sarcasm" raised high—make the absurdity work for you by redirecting the chaos at its creators.

With a little practice, you'll be deflecting nonsense like a pro, and those who try to spew it will learn quickly that they're no match for your powers of sarcasm, distraction, and sheer indifference.

Welcome to the world of surviving bullshit—it's a lot more fun when you don't take it seriously.

Up next: **Feelings.**

Stay tuned. I'll be back after a quick commercial break.

Just kidding, there's no commercial break—it's a book.

Let's have a tea break.

A SATIRICAL MANUAL FOR ADULTS TIRED OF B*LLSH*T

Earth laughs
in flowers.
-Ralph Waldo Emerson

Love, feelings are special. You can pour
some bourbon into your tea if you want.
No judgement.

59

That feeling when there's so much nonsense around that you could draw a Venn diagram with three intersecting categories: workplace, social media, and meetups. At the center: you, with that feeling of way too many feelings or no feelings at all.

That Feeling

Love, I know how you feel. You're tired of bullshit. We all are. I know that feeling.

That feeling when you walk outside and it smells like pee and wet dog blankets and doesn't stop for a whole block.

That feeling when a group at dinner had appetizers, main course, dessert, wine, and espresso and you only had a glass of wine and a salad, but they want to split the bill evenly.

That feeling when you make black tea with bergamot, lemon, and sugar which reminds you of your dormitory days during sophomore year at college. And then you finally come up with what you should have said to someone at work six years ago.

That feeling when you have to be at a social gathering but you'd rather binge Netflix at home. Or vise versa.

That feeling when your "Five more minutes on Instagram" turned into you learning the entire divorce arc of a stranger in Minnesota; and now you know how a cat gives birth at a farm in Dagestan, in detail.

That feeling when you finally get comfortable in bed and then suddenly need to pee, think about your ex, question your entire career path and diet, whether you should start using Botox or get a gun license or cut your hair short or do drum lessons or adopt a baby or take vitamin D.

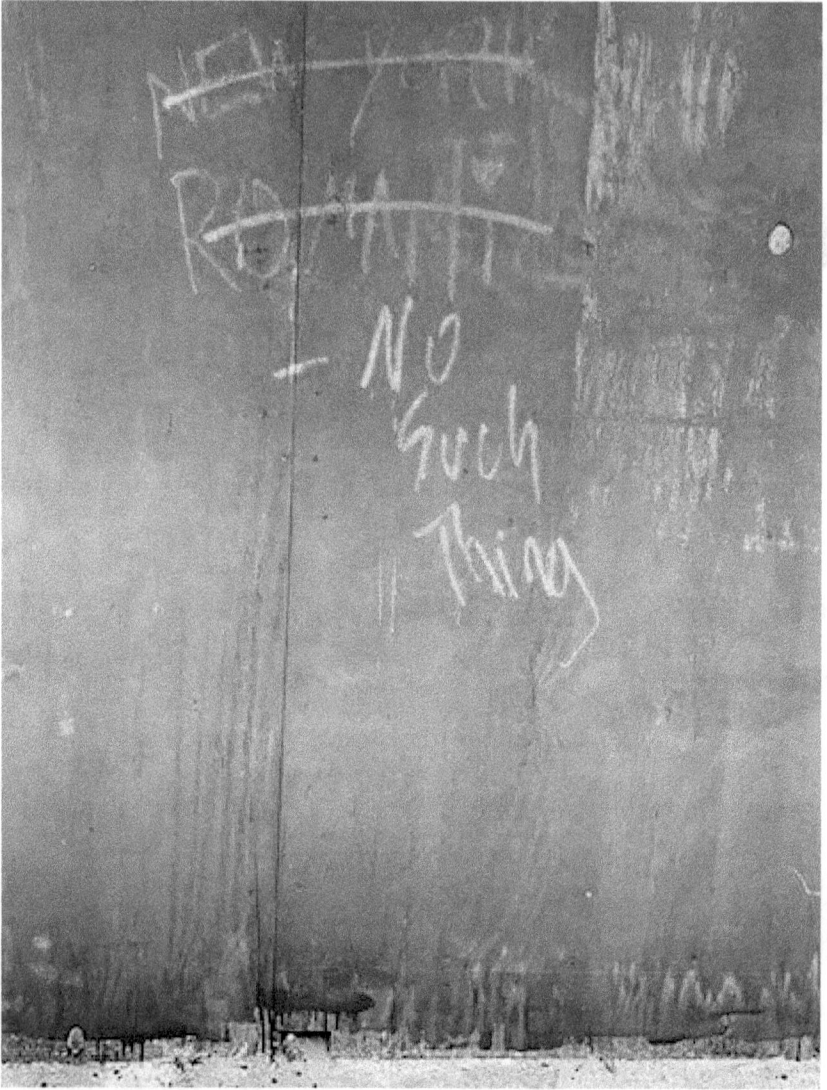

New York romance — no such thing.

Special Addition for NYC

Being a New Yorker is like constantly running an obstacle course, except the obstacles are other people's bad decisions. Trust me, with those absurd rent prices and taxes that make you question your entire existence, New Yorkers need more than just an extra cup of coffee—we need a support group or a hug (preferably free, because, hello!, rent). And if you think you're the only one who feels this way, just know: the BoN has a major office right here in New York, feeding off your frustration.

I'm talking right in the heart of it—somewhere between the guy selling fake Rolexes and a pigeon that just decided it owns the block, the people watching videos out loud on the subway without realizing headphones exist and the slowest walkers in the history of time moving at the speed of a snail on vacation. But you've got bigger fish to fry—like dodging dog poop and rats.

The BoN thrives on the same nonsense that makes you question humanity. The only problem is that New York City makes it the hardest for them to annoy you because they can't hear you over your inner rage, construction site noise, and ambulance siren.

Only in New York do you go out for "just one drink" and somehow end up recounting your entire life story to a stranger named Chad. Is it good? Is it bad? Both. Is it nonsense or soundness? Both.

Survival Tip: make a T-shirt: "If you can survive in New York, you can survive anywhere".

The New Yorker Manual

New York is the best city in the world!

God I hate New York!

New York is the best city in the world!

God I hate New York!

Fuck you! Fuck this! Fuck everything!

Fuck me. Oh, I'm good.

I'm good. I'm good. I'm good. I'm good.

New York is the best city in the world!

New York is the best city in the world!

New York is the best city in the world!

Fuck all this. I gotta leave!

But New York is the best city in the world!

Oh, yeah! I'm good.

If you truly love
nature, you will find
beauty everywhere.
-Vincent van Gogh

Love, have a cup of tea and think
about what the garbage truck
noise at 3 a.m. means, because
everything happens for a reason,
right?

SOMEThing
AWESOME
HAPPENS
TODAY

SOMEThing
AWESOME
HAPPENS
TODAY

Feel Better Techniques

Love, don't roll your eyes. Look, you can even color it if you want. Blue or red would be best. No, I didn't mean it politically. Those colors just look cool. It's not like I called you an elephant or a donkey. No, I don't think you're fat or stupid. No, I don't. Okay... now I doubt it. What? I didn't say anything.

Something Awesome Happens Today.

I know it sounds so tacky that you almost threw up in your mouth a little bit. At least I didn't call it a "mantra" or a "vibe."

What if you just go with it for a day?

Let the universe give you a gift — that something awesome happens today. You deserve it, don't you, Love? Just be sure that something awesome happens today.

And today.

And today.

Just go with the flow.

Embrace the flow.

Be the flow.

SUNSHiNE
STATE OfMiND

SUNSHiNE
STATE OfMiND

SUNSHiNE
STATE OfMiND

SUNSHiNE
STATE OfMiND

Sunshine State of Mind

The next level of the Awesome Technique is Sunshine State of Mind.

Sunshine State of Mind is when you're so happy that other people take offense.

You can color your sunshine state of mind too. Yes, Love, these days you can color pretty much anything and everything if it makes you feel better.

Color your gloomy friends with markers.

Color the White House with felt-tip pens, but only seasonally — every fashionista will tell you the rule: no white color after Labor Day.

Amazon Prime is too slow and you can't take it anymore? Snatch a coloring book from a preschooler — a kid you know or a stranger kid, doesn't matter.

Love, anything for your happiness.

71

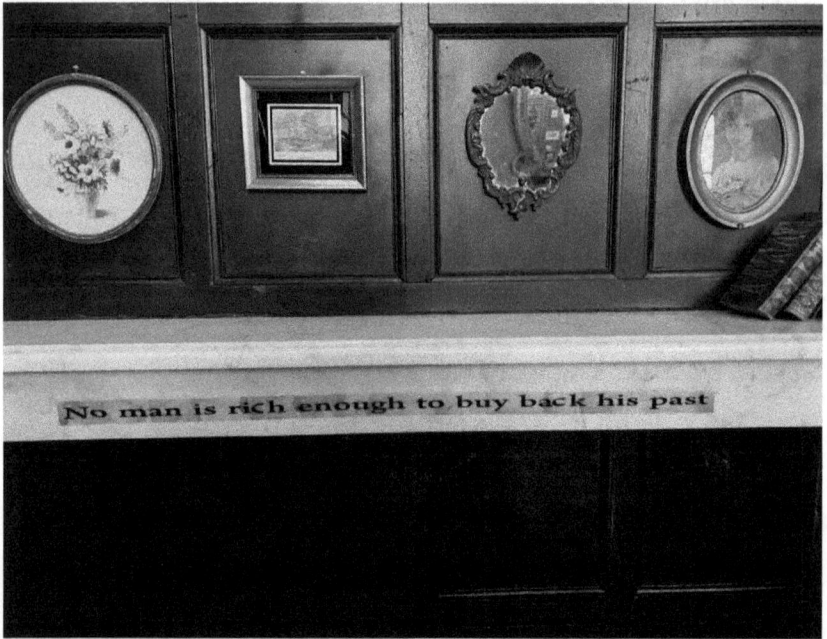

No man is rich enough to buy back his past

The best time is always now.

Nonsense Acceptance

In the face of constant chaos, endless buzzwords, and a world that sometimes feels like it's run by caffeinated toddlers in charge of a room full of dynamite, it's easy to lose your cool. But what if, just for a moment, you could stop fighting it? What if the best way to survive the madness is to embrace the nonsense and just let it wash over you like a peaceful tide?

Karen will karen.

Meetings will be meetings.

The world is on fire—might as well toast marshmallows.

Nonsense acceptance is a practice of choosing not to engage with the daily absurdities that hold no real value in your life.

You can't control what happens around you, but you can control how you react.

By choosing to accept the absurdity instead of fighting it, you gain a power few people understand. You rise above the noise. You find peace in the chaos.

Survival Tip: stop caring!

Sometimes, it is the best way to survive. You only have a limited number of fucks that are actually important. Give out each and every fuck wisely.

Let Go of the Nonsense

Sometimes, the best way to handle the nonsense in your life is to simply let it go. Angry bosses, piles of papers, and screaming influencers—stop.

What if, instead of trying to correct that one coworker who insists on using the phrase "irregardless," you just accepted that this is their reality, and you're not here to fix it?

The person who over-explains the obvious? They're going to keep doing it no matter how many times you raise your hand to point out that we all understand how a stapler works.

The Karen in the supermarket who's convinced the universe is out to get her? She's on her own journey. Don't get bogged down by these daily annoyances.

Let go of the need to be right.

The next time the world feels like it's spinning out of control, remember: let it. You are untouchable.

The universe will still be absurd tomorrow. There's a certain zen to letting go of the need to correct, confront, or even understand the senseless things people say and do.

Survival Tip: accept it and move on!

If you absolutely have to be right, at least charge money for your advice.

The Power of Detachment

Nonsense isn't just in the words we hear; it's in the situations we find ourselves in. How many times have you been dragged into yet another meaningless conversation? Or how many hours have you spent pretending to care about someone's vacation photos while inside you're planning your escape to the nearest exit?

Instead of getting frustrated, detach yourself emotionally from these situations. When someone goes on a long-winded rant about their new pyramid scheme or a dog that can play chess, just nod and mentally check out.

When the world feels out of control, your job is not to solve everything. Your job is to keep going. Find humor where you can. Find peace where it hides. And when all else fails, remember this: you're allowed to be upset about the nonsense *and* enjoy a piece of chocolate on the same day. Life's complicated like that.

Survival Tip: move away and take a look!

When your brain starts to melt from the nonsense in front of you, imagine you're a distant observer in a nature documentary. "Look at this fascinating species," you might say in your mind. "A human in its natural habitat, confusing 'basic' for 'advanced.'"

Breathe Through the Nonsense

Climate change, political drama, pandemics, and that weird colleague who won't stop talking about his homemade kombucha. It's enough to make anyone want to crawl under the bed. But unfortunately, no one's delivering pizza down there.

When the world feels like it's crumbling under the weight of stupidity, there's only one thing to do: breathe. Just take a deep, calming breath and let the absurdity pass through you like a cloud.

The stupidity will still be there after your breath, but you'll find that you've risen above it—untouchable.

Survival Tip: take a deep breath and smile one absurd moment at a time!

Accept that everything is ridiculous and be at peace with that. Sometimes, the real victory is accepting that some things are beyond your control, and that's perfectly fine.

Ignoring the Noise

The modern world is noisy—really noisy. We're constantly bombarded by influencers telling us what to buy, what to believe, and what to say. Social media fills our feeds with outrageous opinions, the 24-hour news cycle through endless nonsense, and Instagram experts have more advice than we know what to do with. And all of it is pure nonsense.

Tune out that noise.

Imagine it like a soothing white noise machine, but instead of the sound of ocean waves, it's the constant hum of irrelevant opinions and unqualified experts. You don't have to engage. You don't have to argue. Simply turn down the volume and let the chaos continue on its merry way. It's like standing in the middle of a highway during rush hour, with the cars whizzing by you at top speed. Everyone else is frantically driving in circles, but you're just standing there, unfazed, letting the world move around you.

In pursuit of relaxation, don't let true self-care become the buzzword. Live the care. Give yourself permission to take the day off. But don't announce it with a hashtag like #MentalHealthDay. And replace "detox" teas with water, the original detox. Real self-care is about saying *no*, not buying *more*.

Survival Tip: You don't need a $300 crystal lamp to find peace. Try a nap. It's free and has a 100% success rate for tired people.

Zen Exercise

Let's take this Zen concept to a whole new level with an exercise you can do anytime you feel your blood pressure rising: picture in full meditation pose, in the center of a giant, glowing bubble of calm.

C'mon, Love, everything has to be glowing these days—that is the trend. What did you say? You heard it as "a giant, glowing bubble of cum"? Sure. Why not at this point. Whatever works for you, Love.

Visualize this bubble as a safe, impenetrable space. Yes, impenetrable by cum. Outside the bubble, the world is chaos. But inside your bubble, you are untouchable by the madness swirling around.

Feel the absurdity outside your bubble, but let it bounce off. You have no obligation to respond, react, or even acknowledge it.

Focus on your breath. Inhale deeply, hold it for a second, and then slowly exhale. With each breath, let the noise of the outside world fade a little more.

You are at peace. You are beyond the noise.

Repeat. Whenever the world becomes too much, return to your bubble of calm. Picture it in your mind, feel the peace within it, and let the chaos swirl on without your involvement.

You know what they say, Love: your bubble—your rules.

Bureaucratic Infinite Loop. You Came Here From Page 121

"HR says this isn't their jurisdiction. Maybe Legal?"

To continue reading this paragraph, please go to **page 30** and follow the instructions there.

Feel Better Activities

1. Come to the mirror in the bathroom, look at your reflection, and say loud and clear: "Calm the Fuck Down." Keep looking yourself in the eyes and repeat it eight times, or until the necessary calmness is achieved. Calm the Fuck Down technique doesn't work on others, especially on women, especially if you're a man applying that technique. To this day, scientists don't know why, but Calm the Fuck Down technique provides the opposite effect when applied to others. Works only on yourself.

2. Close your eyes and imagine you're on a tropical island — without Wi-Fi. Now open your eyes, panic, and run around like Calkin in Home Alone (Part 1 obviously, the original one, duh!) until complete exhaustion. Pro tip: run around with closed eyes.

3. Go to the nearest park with swings and swing until you feel better, or nauseous.

4. Maybe instead of trying goat yoga in a steam room filled with puppies who have personal chiropractors, you could try... sitting quietly for five minutes and thinking about literally nothing.

5. Acknowledge the need for work-life balance. Consider leaving your job. Do not, under any circumstances, open your bank app to check the balance. Just live with the thought that you've resigned for a while. You'll deal with reality later, when you miss food.

6. You've got this, probably. And you've got two options: sob uncontrollably or laugh until you can't breathe. Personally, I recommend the latter.

7. In any crazy situation, clean the floors. You'll feel better afterwards.

8. Meal prep something simple and nourishing. Maybe it's just spaghetti. Maybe it's cereal for dinner. Who cares? You've eaten. Gold star for you.

9. Tidy one corner of your space. No need to deep clean. Just relocate the dirty sock glaring at you from under the bed you wanted to crawl under before. See? Instant improvement.

10. Take a shower and pretend you're in a perfume commercial. Glamorous, over-the-top narration optional.

11. Dance in your kitchen in mismatched socks. Or naked. Preferably to ABBA's "Dancing Queen" song. No scientific studies — just trust me on this song.

12. Don't do affirmations. Love yourself. It's the only one that actually works.

13. Finally tell that someone whatever you're holding in — good or bad — say it.

YOU'RE GOING TO WANT TO GIVE UP.

DON'T!

Okay, Love! It's time to feel better.
Do you feel it?

Feel Better Technique. International Addition

If you deal with people globally, it's useful to know the main magic words in all the official languages of the United Nations: English, Russian, French, Spanish, Arabic, and Chinese. Five phrases to get you through the work week, consisting of:

Denial

Anger

Bargaining

Depression

Acceptance

Saturday (you're happy here)

Sunday (and here)

Because cursing is caring.
And sharing is caring.
Share the curse — be a good person.

English: **What the fuck?**

Russian: Что за хуйня? **Chto za khui nya?**
What the fuck?

French: Putain, c'est quoi ce bordel?
Poo tan say kwa suh bor del?
What the fuck is going on?

Spanish: ¿Qué coño pasa? **Keh koh nyo pah sah?**
What the fuck is happening?

Arabic: إيش هذا اللعنة؟ **Ish hadha al la'na?**
What the curse is this?

Chinese: 他妈的，怎么回事? **Ta ma de, zen me hui shi?**
What the fuck is going on?

English: **Shut the fuck up!**

Russian: Заткнись, сука! **Zat knis soo ka!**
Shut up, bitch!

French: Ferme ta putain de gueule! Shut the fuck up!
Fairm ta poo tan duh guhl!

Spanish: ¡Cállate la puta boca! **Kah ya teh la poo ta bo ka!**
Shut your fucking mouth.

Arabic: اخرس يا كلب! **Ukh ros ya kalb!**
Shut up, dog!

Chinese: 你闭嘴，傻逼! **Ni bee zway sha bee!**
Shut up, stupid cunt!

English: **You son of a bitch!**

Russian: Ты, сука! **Ty soo ka!**
You, bitch!

French: Espèce de salaud! **Es pess duh sah lo!**
You bastard!

Spanish: ¡Hijo de puta! **Ee ho de poo ta!**
Son of a bitch!

Arabic: ابن العاهرة! **Ibn al aahira!**
Son of a whore!

Chinese: 你这个王八蛋 ! **Ni juh guh wahng ba dan!**
You son of a bitch! / You bastard!

English: **You're a fucking asshole.**

Russian: Ты мудак! **Ty ye ba nui moo dak!**
You asshole!

French: T'es qu'un con! **Teh kuh kohn!**
You're such an idiot!

Spanish: Eres un cabrón. **Eh res oon kah bronn.**
You're an asshole.

Arabic: أنت حمار! **Anta himar!**
You donkey! (meaning "You idiot!")

Chinese: 你个傻逼! **Ni guh sha bee!**
You fucking idiot!

English: **Go fuck yourself.**

Russian: Иди на хуй! **Ee dee na khui!**
Go fuck yourself!

French: Va te faire enculer! **Va tuh fehr ahn koo lay!**
Go fuck yourself!

Spanish: ¡Que te jodan! **Keh teh hoh dan!**
Fuck you.

Arabic: إذهب إلى الجحيم! **Izh hab ila al ja heem!**
Go to hell!

Chinese: 操你! **Cao ni!**
Fuck you!

The **Universal Language of Nonsense**

At some point, we all have to be a part of nonsense and knowing its language can be very helpful, especially at board meetings, political speeches and other office gatherings where you're meant to sit, listen, and suffer. By randomly combining parts of a phrase from column 1 with any part of the phrase sequentially from columns 2, 3, and 4, you will create a universal text of 10,000 combinations, which is enough for a 40-minute speech.

1	2	3	4
Ladies and Gentlemen!	the implementation of the planned objectives	plays an important role in shaping	the existing financial and administrative conditions.
On the other hand,	the framework and place of training personnel	requires us to analyze	the further directions of development.
Similarly,	the constant quantitative growth and the scope of our activity	requires the definition and clarification of	the mass participation system.
However, it should not be forgotten that	the established organizational structure	contributes to the preparation and implementation of	the positions held by participants in relation to the assigned tasks.

1	2	3	4
Thus,	the new model of organizational activity	ensures the participation of a wide range of specialists in the formation of	new proposals.
Everyday practice shows that	the further development of various forms of activity	allows for the completion of important tasks related to the development of	progressive development directions.
The importance of these issues is so evident that	the constant informational support of our activities	largely determines the creation of	a training system for personnel that meets urgent needs.
The diverse and rich experience of	strengthening and developing the structure	allows us to assess the importance of	the corresponding conditions for activation.
The task of the organization, especially	the consultation with a broad active group	represents an interesting experiment in testing of	the development model.
The idea of a higher order, as well as	the initiation of daily work on shaping a position	entails the process of implementation and modernization of	methods of influence.

Use this instead of a crystal ball.

Decision Help Technique

For those times when you can't dare to do something, use this as a green light.

For those times when deciding on something becomes a custom-made torture.

For those times when you want to talk to someone but don't actually want to talk.

For those times when you remember that you have only one life.

It's better to do something and regret it than not do it and regret it later.

Love, live life a little!

Anti-Stress Technique

Color the words... or just spit on them if you don't have any crayons. Options for different colors can be spit after a sip of black coffee, after eating cherries/strawberries/beets, if you've been smoking for way too long, or go couleur naturel.

After this anti-stress coloring book, you will instantly feel better. Your problems won't go away, but you'll feel better for sure. Trust me, Love.

These are the best seven words according to George Carlin and humanity. The lucky seven: shit, piss, fuck, cunt, cocksucker, motherfucker, tits.

SHIT

SHIT

SHIT

SHIT

SHIT

SHIT

SHIT

SHIT

SHIT

SHIT

SHITSHIT

SHITSHIT

SHITSHIT

SHITSHIT

SHITSHIT

SHITSHIT

SHITSHIT

SHITSHIT

SHITSHIT

SHITSHIT

SHITSHIT

SHITSHIT

SHITSHIT

SHITSHIT

SHITSHIT

SHITSHIT

PISS

PISS

PISS

PISS

PISS

PISS

PISS

PISS

PISS

PISS

A SATIRICAL MANUAL FOR ADULTS TIRED OF B*LLSH*T

PISSPISS

PISSPISS

PISSPISS

PISSPISS

PISSPISS

PISSPISS

PISSPISS

PISSPISS

PISSPISS

PISSPISS

PISSPISS

PISSPISS

PISSPISS

PISSPISS

PISSPISS

PISSPISS

FUCK

FUCK

FUCK

FUCK

FUCK

FUCK

FUCK

FUCK

FUCK

FUCK

FUCK

FUCK

FUCKFUCK

FUCKFUCK

FUCKFUCK

FUCKFUCK

FUCKFUCK

FUCKFUCK

FUCKFUCK

FUCKFUCK

FUCKFUCK

FUCKFUCK

FUCKFUCK

FUCKFUCK

FUCKFUCK

FUCKFUCK

FUCKFUCK

FUCKFUCK

FUCKFUCK

FUCKFUCK

A SATIRICAL MANUAL FOR ADULTS TIRED OF B*LLSH*T

CUNT
CUNT
CUNT
CUNT
CUNT
CUNT

CUNT

CUNT

CUNT

CUNT

CUNT

CUNT

CUNTCUNT

CUNTCUNT

CUNTCUNT

CUNTCUNT

CUNTCUNT

CUNTCUNT

CUNTCUNT

CUNTCUNT

CUNTCUNT

CUNTCUNT

CUNTCUNT

CUNTCUNT

CUNTCUNT

CUNTCUNT

CUNTCUNT

CUNTCUNT

CUNTCUNT

CUNTCUNT

COCK

SUCKER

COCK

SUCKER

COCK

SUCKER

COCK

SUCKER

COCK
SUCKER
COCK
SUCKER
COCK
SUCKER
COCK
SUCKER

A SATIRICAL MANUAL FOR ADULTS TIRED OF B*LLSH*T

COCKSUCKER

COCKSUCKER

COCKSUCKER

COCKSUCKER

COCKSUCKER

COCKSUCKER

COCKSUCKER

COCKSUCKER

COCKSUCKER

COCKSUCKER

COCKSUCKER

COCKSUCKER

COCKSUCKER

COCKSUCKER

COCKSUCKER

COCKSUCKER

COCKSUCKER

COCKSUCKER

COCKSUCKER

COCKSUCKER

COCKSUCKER

COCKSUCKER

MOTHER
FUCKER
MOTHER
FUCKER
MOTHER
FUCKER
MOTHER
FUCKER

MOTHER
FUCKER
MOTHER
FUCKER
MOTHER
FUCKER
MOTHER
FUCKER

MOTHERFUCKER

MOTHERFUCKER

MOTHERFUCKER

MOTHERFUCKER

MOTHERFUCKER

MOTHERFUCKER

MOTHERFUCKER

MOTHERFUCKER

MOTHERFUCKER

MOTHERFUCKER

MOTHERFUCKER

MOTHERFUCKER

MOTHERFUCKER

MOTHERFUCKER

MOTHERFUCKER

MOTHERFUCKER

MOTHERFUCKER

MOTHERFUCKER

MOTHERFUCKER

MOTHERFUCKER

MOTHERFUCKER

MOTHERFUCKER

MOTHERFUCKER

MOTHERFUCKER

TITS

TITS

TITS

TITS

TITS

TITS

TITS

TITS

TITS

TITS

A SATIRICAL MANUAL FOR ADULTS TIRED OF B*LLSH*T

TITSTITS

TITSTITS

TITSTITS

TITSTITS

TITSTITS

TITSTITS

TITSTITS

TITSTITS

TITSTITS

TITSTITS

TITSTITS

TITSTITS

TITSTITS

TITSTITS

Bureaucratic Infinite Loop. You Came Here From Page 30

"Susan? Oh no, she's on maternity leave. Try Mike in HR."

To continue reading this paragraph, please go to **page 79** and follow the instructions there.

Positive Coloring Technique

Color the words and you will instantly feel better. Your problems won't go away, but you'll feel better for sure. Trust me, Love.

I know, we needed an extra page for cursing words before, but here it's only three pages per word. Because you are only half-stressed at this point after the anti-stress coloring book.

Here are great eight adjectives for adults needing a boost. You are all those beautiful adjectives, Love.

Now get to coloring, bitch!

Get happy!

I said, get happy!

Now!

A SATIRICAL MANUAL FOR ADULTS TIRED OF B*LLSH*T

HONEST

HONEST

HONEST

HONEST

HONEST

HONEST

HONEST

HONEST

HONEST

HONEST

HONEST

HONEST

HONEST

HONEST

A SATIRICAL MANUAL FOR ADULTS TIRED OF B*LLSH*T

HONESTHONEST

HONESTHONEST

HONESTHONEST

HONESTHONEST

HONESTHONEST

HONESTHONEST

HONESTHONEST

HONESTHONEST

HONESTHONEST

HONESTHONEST

HONESTHONEST

HONESTHONEST

SMART

SMART

SMART

SMART

SMART

SMART

SMART

SMART

SMART

SMART

SMART

SMART

SMART

SMART

SMARTSMART

SMARTSMART

SMARTSMART

SMARTSMART

SMARTSMART

SMARTSMART

SMARTSMART

SMARTSMART

SMARTSMART

SMARTSMART

SMARTSMART

BEAU
TIFUL

BEAU
TIFUL

BEAU
TIFUL

BEAU
TIFUL

BEAU
TIFUL

BEAU
TIFUL

BEAU
TIFUL

BEAU
TIFUL

A SATIRICAL MANUAL FOR ADULTS TIRED OF B*LLSH*T

BEAUTIFUL

BEAUTIFUL

BEAUTIFUL

BEAUTIFUL

BEAUTIFUL

BEAUTIFUL

BEAUTIFUL

BEAUTIFUL

BEAUTIFUL

BEAUTIFUL

BEAUTIFUL

FUNNY

FUNNY

FUNNY

FUNNY

FUNNY

FUNNY

FUNNY

FUNNY

FUNNY

FUNNY

FUNNY

FUNNY

FUNNY

FUNNY

FUNNYFUNNY

FUNNYFUNNY

FUNNYFUNNY

FUNNYFUNNY

FUNNYFUNNY

FUNNYFUNNY

FUNNYFUNNY

FUNNYFUNNY

FUNNYFUNNY

FUNNYFUNNY

STRONG

STRONG

STRONG

STRONG

STRONG

STRONG

STRONG

STRONG

STRONG

STRONG

STRONG

STRONG

STRONG

STRONG

STRONG

STRONG

STRONGSTRONG

STRONGSTRONG

STRONGSTRONG

STRONGSTRONG

STRONGSTRONG

STRONGSTRONG

STRONGSTRONG

STRONGSTRONG

STRONGSTRONG

STRONGSTRONG

STRONGSTRONG

STRONGSTRONG

STRONGSTRONG

KIND

KIND

KIND

KIND

KIND

KIND

KIND

KIND

KIND

KIND

KINDKIND

KINDKIND

KINDKIND

KINDKIND

KINDKIND

KINDKIND

KINDKIND

KINDKIND

CARING

CARING

CARING

CARING

CARING

CARING

CARING

CARING

CARING

CARING

CARING

CARING

CARING

CARING

CARINGCARING

CARINGCARING

CARINGCARING

CARINGCARING

CARINGCARING

CARINGCARING

CARINGCARING

CARINGCARING

CARINGCARING

CARINGCARING

CARINGCARING

CONFIDENT

CONFIDENT

CONFIDENT

CONFIDENT

CONFIDENT

CONFIDENT

CONFIDENT

CONFIDENT

CONFIDENT

CONFIDENT

CONFIDENT

CONFIDENT

CONFIDENT

CONFIDENT

CONFIDENT

CONFIDENT

CONFIDENT

CONFIDENT

CONFIDENT

CONFIDENT

CONFIDENT

CONFIDENT

CONFIDENT

CONFIDENT

CONFIDENT

CONFIDENT

CONFIDENT

STYLISH
SMART
SILLY
FABULOUS

You are, Love! I'm so proud of you!

The World Is on Fire So What's for Dinner?

Congratulations!

You've reached zen.

Hope it was all you, and not booze or pharmaceuticals allowed only by a doctor's prescription.

Now that you've mastered all the techniques, you are ready for the final round: becoming the Master of Nonsense Deflection.

One touch of
nature makes the
whole world kin.
-William Shakespeare

Love, you've had so many cups of
calming chamomile tea — you are
ready for anything. You can do it!

Nonsense Deflection

You've learned how to fight the BoN, but it's time to level up and become an unstoppable force of indifference. In the final stage of this war, the true weapon is not fighting back—it's walking away with a sense of smug satisfaction. The BoN is about reaction. If you don't react, they lose their power.

Here's your toolkit for mastering the art of nonsense deflection:

The "I'm Too Tired for This" Face. Think you're too stressed to care? Perfect. The more done you feel, the better this works. Your job here is to look like you've been dragged through the chaos of hell, like you've seen way too much already, like you've seen the darkest corners of the darknet and that still didn't scare you. Throw in a sigh so heavy it could create a seismic wave. And if anyone keeps talking to you, give them another ambiguous sign for an answer.

The Power of the Walkaway. There will come a moment when you're sitting in a meeting, and someone says, "Let's circle back to this," or you're at a party that is so boring you can hear your nails grow, or a BoN agent is onto you through Karens. Don't make a fuss. Just grab your stuff and walk out. Don't say a word. Don't give them the satisfaction of acknowledging that you're done. Leave the party early. When you do what you want, you're sending a message: they can't control someone who doesn't care about their nonsense.

Humor as a Weapon and Shield. From mysterious smiles to sarcastic punchlines on time, laughter is your best friend.

Joining the Resistance

If you think you're alone in this battle, think again. There's a whole underground network of people who, like you, are tired of the BoN's nonsense. The key to victory lies in unity. Find and identify allies in the wild who are sick of the nonsense, and together you can create an unstoppable force—one that understands that the true power lies in not caring.

Secret Handshakes. The next time you meet someone who's had enough of the BoN's nonsense, don't shake their hand like everyone else. No, that's *what they want*. Instead, develop a secret handshake that involves awkward hand gestures and an overly dramatic handshake. Bonus points if you throw in a jazz hands move or a spontaneous high-five followed by a full somersault.

Nonsense-Free Zones. It's time to create sanctuaries of sanity in this chaotic world. Maybe it's a corner of the office, a hidden bench in the break room, or even the backseat of a car parked in a secluded spot. In these zones, buzzwords and jargon are strictly prohibited. If someone dares to utter, "Can we pivot on that?" immediately shout, "No pivoting! We're not getting paid enough for that!"

Pranking the Nonsense Spreaders. The best way to fight back against the BoN is with pranks. Replace every corporate buzzword poster with one that says, "Nothing Matters, Go Home" in large, bold letters. Or, swap the motivational posters with one that reads, "Pretend You're Busy Until the Day Is Over." Watch as the BoN employees, who take their buzzwords like religion, crumble in confusion.

You're building an army of anti-nonsense rebels—and you've got to be sneaky. Even your rallying cry sounds less like a protest and more like a late-night comedy show. The BoN never expects a resistance made up of people who enjoy sarcasm and snacks.

Office Nonsense. What if we replaced all meetings with interpretive dance? Picture the CEO giving a quarterly update through interpretive dance, while the entire staff solemnly nods. When someone suggests a PowerPoint, you respond with, "Great, can we have a hologram too? Maybe a llama in a tutu?" You'll soon see the very essence of "business professionalism" crumble under the weight of your ridiculousness. Your boss emailed you at 11 p.m.? Reply at 2 a.m. with: "Thanks! Let me know when you're free for a Zoom."

Social Media Nonsense. The BoN thrives on making even the most mundane activities seem like earth-shattering events. So, why not join in and overdo it? The next time someone posts a photo of their oatmeal, leave a comment like, "So brave. Truly revolutionary. This is the content we all need in our lives." Every post becomes a chance to pump the nonsense to a hundred. Someone's having a salad for lunch? Comment, "This is why I wake up every day. You're a hero."

Survival Tip: recruit and unite!

Find other nonsense survivors and form a coalition. Your slogan on a poster could say "Not My Circus. Nothing Matters. Go Home."

Nonsense-Proof

Ah, the BoN—an organization fueled by nonsense and powered by the belief that, if they say it with enough authority, it becomes true. Your mission, should you choose to accept it: expose their absurdity for what it is, and do so in such a ludicrous way that even the BoN agents question their existence. The BoN thrives on people taking nonsense seriously. Your mission? Don't.

If they want to drown you in their absurdity, return the favor by making their nonsense even more absurd. It's like playing chess with a toddler—except the toddler is also a mime and has seventeen different hats. You are the epitome of nonsense-proof. BoN agents will be like mosquitoes, buzzing around you, but no matter how hard they try, they'll never land.

You've done it. You've exposed the BoN for what they are: a bunch of overinflated, self-important buffoons who can't function without people taking their nonsense seriously. By walking away, laughing, and never engaging with their empty jargon, you've become a legend in the fight against absurdity.

The BoN's greatest fear is that you'll just stop caring—and that's exactly what you did. You've made their absurdity your comedy, their chaos your normal, and their nonsense your punchline.

Reveal the BoN's greatest fear: people who don't care anymore. When you laugh at their nonsense, they lose their power.

The world might still be ridiculous, but now you're ridiculous enough to handle it and enjoy it your way.

The joke's on them.

Customize Nonsense

Remember Nonsense from the cover? Now is your chance to customize your Nonsense. They say that once you face your Nonsense and deal with it and then laugh at it — it'll disappear.

Hi, I'm Nonsense from the cover.

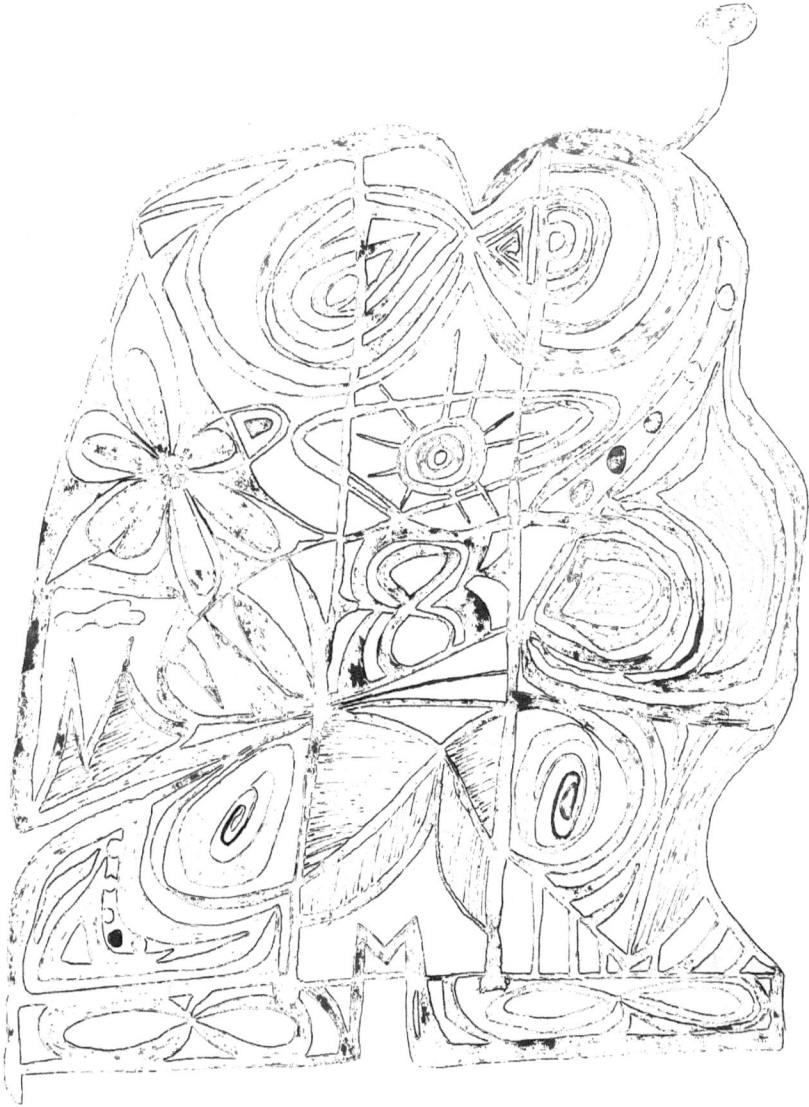

The Unicorn Philosophy

Love, you did a great job satirically dissecting nonsense.

I'm going to be completely honest with you: I didn't want to tell you right away, but now that you're ready and equipped with the survival manual…

Love, it gets way worse. In fact, it's not just the BoN. It's actually *The Bureau of Nonsense,* the *Ministry of Morons,* and the *Bullshit Institute*—the so-called holy trinity. Amen.

Sometimes you fuck the unicorn,

sometimes the unicorn fucks you.

And that's life.

And it's okay.

There's no right or wrong.

Think philosophically.

Enjoy it while you can,

either way.

Laugh. That is the only way.

The cycle of life.

PSST...
IF ANYONE
CATCHES YOU IN
NONSENSE,
NEVER ADMIT
ANYTHING! DENY
EVERYTHING!
THIS IS HOW
NONSENSE STAYS
ALIVE...

Sincerely,
The BoN Agent

www.ingramcontent.com/pod-product-compliance
Lightning Source LLC
Chambersburg PA
CBHW052134270326
41930CB00012B/2883